What Is My Sport?

Diana Noonan

Sport is **good** to do!

This is the ball.

This is my top.

These are the stumps.

This is the bat.

What is my sport?

My sport is cricket.
I play in a team.

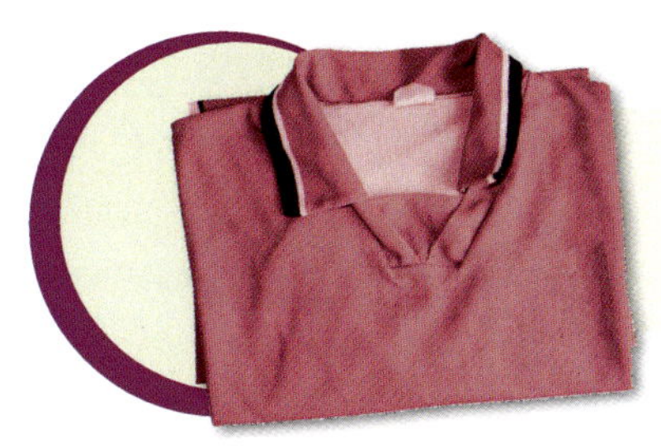

This is my top.

These are my boots.

This is the ball.

This is the net.

What is my sport?

My sport is soccer.
I play in a team.

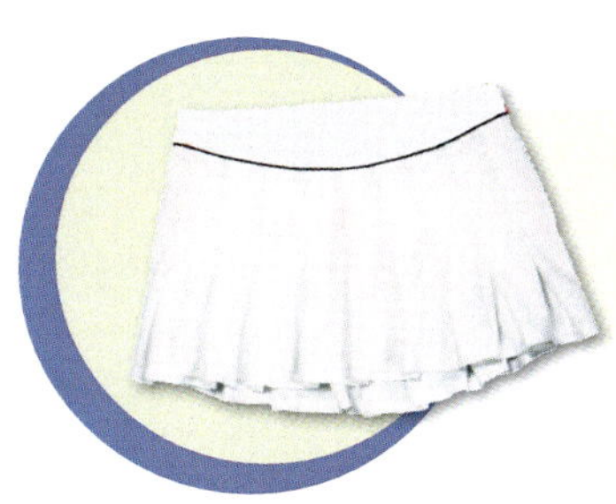

This is my skirt.

These are my shoes.

This is my racket.

This is the ball.

What is my sport?

My sport is tennis.
I play it with my friend.
This is me!

This is my top.

These are my shorts.

These are my shoes.

This is the ball.

What is my sport?

My sport is basketball.
I play in a team.

This is my top.

These are my shorts.

These are my shoes.

What is my sport?

My sport is running.
I run with my friends.

This is my leotard.

This is the mat.

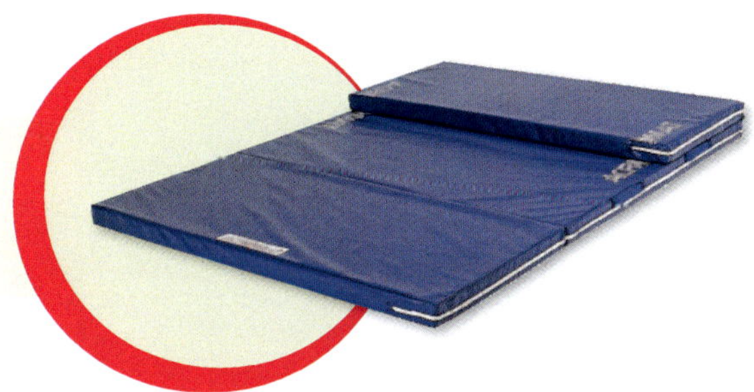

What is my sport?

My sport is gymnastics.
I am in a team.

It is **fun** to do sport!

Index